I Can Write
Diaries

Anita Ganeri

www.raintreepublishers.co.uk
Visit our website to find out more information about Raintree books.

To order:
☎ Phone 0845 6044371
📄 Fax +44 (0) 1865 312263
✉ Email myorders@raintreepublishers.co.uk

Customers from outside the UK please telephone +44 1865 312262

Raintree is an imprint of Capstone Global Library Limited, a company incorporated in England and Wales having its registered office at 7 Pilgrim Street, London, EC4V 6LB – Registered company number: 6695582

Text © Capstone Global Library Limited 2013
First published in hardback in 2013
First published in paperback in 2013
The moral rights of the proprietor have been asserted.

Edited by Daniel Nunn, Rebecca Rissman, and Sian Smith
Designed by Victoria Allen
Picture research by Elizabeth Alexander
Original illustrations © Capstone Global Library Ltd 2013
Illustrated by Victoria Allen and Darren Lingard
Production by Victoria Fitzgerald
Originated by Capstone Global Library Ltd
Printed and bound in China by Leo Paper Products Ltd

ISBN 978 1 406 23830 3 (hardback)
16 15 14 13 12
10 9 8 7 6 5 4 3 2 1

ISBN 978 1 406 23837 2 (paperback)
17 16 15 14 13
10 9 8 7 6 5 4 3 2 1

British Library Cataloguing in Publication Data
Ganeri, Anita, 1961-
  Diaries. -- (I can write)
  1. Diaries--Juvenile literature. 2. Diaries--Authorship--Juvenile literature.
  I. Title II. Series
  808'.06692-dc23

Acknowledgements
We would like to thank the following for permission to reproduce photographs and artworks: Alamy p.5 (© Roberto Herrett); Dreamstime.com p.9 (© Newlight); iStockphoto p.10 (© Joris van Caspel); Shutterstock pp.4 (© OtnaYdur), 8 (© Feng Yu), 11 (© muzsy), 13 (© mates), 14, 15 (© olillia), 16 (© Cory Thoman), 17 (© Anatema), 18, 19 (© MisterElements), 19 (© zhanna ocheret), 21 (© irin-k), 23 (© McVector's), 24 (© rolfik), 24 (© studio BM), 25 (© vectomart), 26-27 (© Yulia M.), 26-27 (© Jana Guothova); Superstock pp.6 (© Universal Images Group), 7 (© Culver Pictures, Inc.).

Every effort has been made to contact copyright holders of material reproduced in this book. Any omissions will be rectified in subsequent printings if notice is given to the publisher.

Contents

Some words are shown in bold, **like this**. You can find out what they mean in the glossary on page 30.

What is writing?

When you put words on paper or on a computer screen, you are being a writer. You need to write clearly so that readers can understand what you mean.

What do you like writing about?

Writing a diary can be fun.

There are many different types of writing. This book is about diaries and **recounts**. Diaries and recounts are a type of **non-fiction**. This means that they are about real facts.

What is a diary?

A diary is a book. In it, you write down what happens to you every day. You also write down how you felt or what you thought about the things that happened.

Samuel Pepys lived hundreds of years ago. We know about his life because he kept a diary.

Anne Frank wrote a diary during World War II.

In a diary, you write things down in the order in which they happened. This is called **chronological** order. People keep diaries to help them remember what happened.

Lots of diaries

There are lots of different types of diaries. Some people jot down **appointments** in a diary. Some people write a diary of what they do every day.

This is an appointments diary.

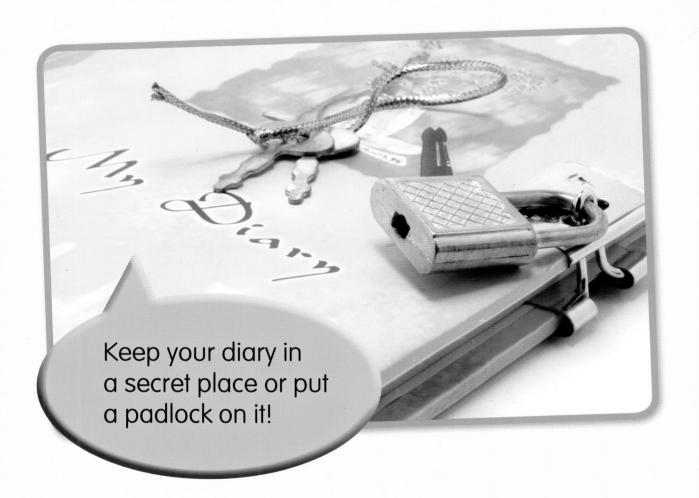

Keep your diary in a secret place or put a padlock on it!

You might keep a diary when you are on holiday so that you can remember the good times you had. Some diaries are top secret. Everyone else has to KEEP OUT!

Keeping a diary

Try keeping a diary for a week. Write down what you do every day. Don't forget to write in the days and dates. This will help you to remember when things happened.

What did you do today? Write it in your diary.

What other exciting things did you do this week?

At the end of the week, read your diary back to yourself. Pick out the most interesting or important things that you did. Did you play football or go to a party? What did you do at the weekend?

Writing style

Write your diary in the **first person** because you are writing about yourself. This means using the **pronoun** 'I'.
You can use the pronoun 'we' if you are writing about you and other people.

I went to a birthday party.

'I' and 'we' are first person pronouns.

Use the **past tense** in your diary. This is because you are talking about things that have already happened.

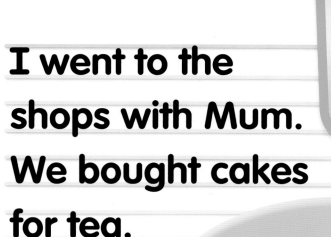

I went to the shops with Mum. We bought cakes for tea.

'Went' and 'bought' are the past tenses of the **verbs** 'to go' and 'to buy'.

Diary language

When you are writing your diary, don't just write down what happened. You can also write down your feelings or thoughts. This will make your diary more interesting.

Today, we went to the zoo. The monkeys were brilliant. I loved watching them swing through the trees.

What else did you like about the monkeys?

Write down things in the order that they happened. You can use words or phrases called **time connectives** to help you. Look at this list of time connectives.

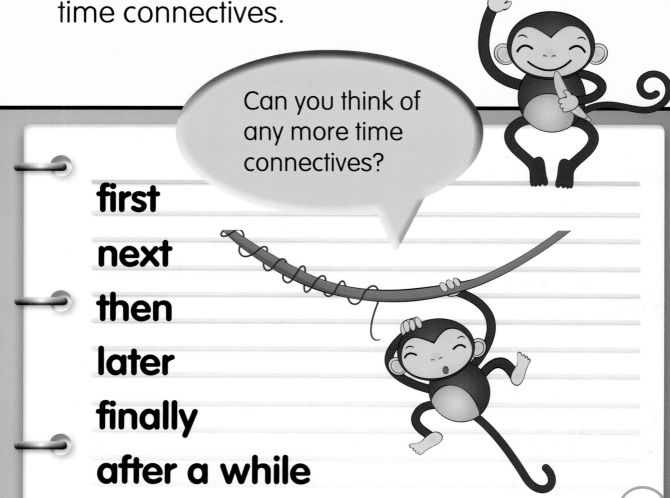

Can you think of any more time connectives?

first

next

then

later

finally

after a while

Pet's diary

Imagine if your pet could keep a diary. What would it write? Here are some **sentences** to get you started. These are for a dog's diary. Can you write them out in the correct order?

I chased some ducks.
I went home and
went to sleep.
We went to the park.

Can you add some **time connectives**, too?

Try it out for yourself! Pretend that you are a pet cat or dog. Keep a diary of what you do for a week. It might start off something like this:

Use full sentences to make your writing clear.

Dog's diary

Monday

I went to the vet's for a check-up.

Tuesday

I played with a new toy.

Astronaut's diary

Imagine that you are an astronaut. You are about to blast off into space on your way to the Moon. Keep a diary of your trip. Here are some **sentences** to start you off.

What could you write next?

At last, it was time for the countdown –

10, 9, 8, 7, 6, 5, 4, 3, 2, 1. We blasted off into space. It was so exciting…

Try to think about how you are feeling as you blast off. Add some details about the spaceship and who else is travelling with you.

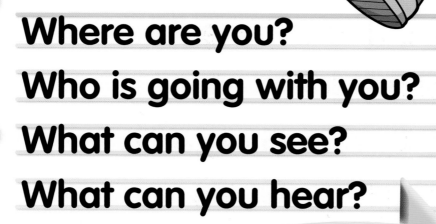

Where are you?

Who is going with you?

What can you see?

What can you hear?

Here are some questions to ask yourself.

Writing a blog

A **blog** is a type of diary that you write **online** on the internet. You write it every day. Each time you write something, it is called a post. Each post is usually quite short.

Had a brilliant time today! Scored three times in a football match.

You can use **informal** writing for blogs. That is language that is casual and friendly.

Ask your teacher if you can write a class blog. Write posts of what your class does every day. Your teacher might put your blog on the school website.

Never give any information such as your name, address, or email address in a blog.

Got our new topic today.

We're finding out about minibeasts.

They are interesting animals.

This is a beetle.

What is a recount?

A **recount** is a piece of writing which describes an event that happened in the past. The event might be something such as a school trip or family outing.

Here are some things to remember when you are writing a recount.

Recount checklist

- **Snappy title?**
- **First person?**
- **Past tense?**
- **Time connectives?**

In a recount, remember to say what happened, when it happened, why it happened, and where it happened. For short, try to remember: What? When? Why? Where?

You can make your writing interesting by explaining how you felt.

On Saturday, I went to the seaside. It was my brother's birthday. I woke him up early because I was excited.

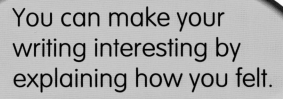

Planning a recount

Before you start writing, you need to plan your **recount**. Start with an **introduction**. It needs to set the scene and tell the reader what your recount is about.

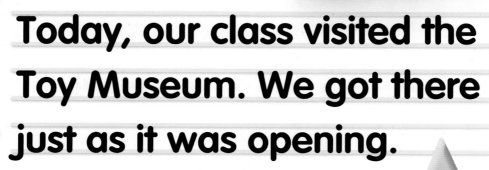

Today, our class visited the Toy Museum. We got there just as it was opening.

The introduction tells the reader where you are.

Write things in **chronological** order.
Divide your recount into **paragraphs**
to make it easier to read. Add
a **sentence** at the end to tell the
reader what happened.

The ending pulls everything together.

After the visit, we got the bus back to school. We all had a great day!

Timelines and ladders

It can be tricky to remember events in the right order. You can draw a **timeline** to help you. Then write down the events in order, from start to finish.

Write down the main events as notes.

Birthday timeline

got up – opened presents – picnic – trip to zoo – birthday dinner

You could also put the events on a ladder, like the one below. Start at the bottom of the ladder and work your way up to the top.

You can add more rungs to your ladder if you want.

Birthday ladder

birthday dinner

trip to zoo

picnic

opened presents

got up

Tips for writing diaries and recounts

1. Read lots of different diaries and **recounts**. The more you read, the better your own writing will become.

2. Read through your diary or recount when you have finished. Check your spelling and correct anything that is wrong.

3. Remember to write the date on each page of your diary so that you know when things happened.

4. If your diary is secret, you can use notes and **informal** language. If it is for your teacher or parents, use a more **formal** writing style.

5. Remember to add your own thoughts and feelings. This will make your writing more interesting.

6. Use lots of **adjectives** (describing words) and strong **verbs** (doing words) in your writing. These will help your reader to imagine how you felt.

7. If you get stuck for ideas, try some automatic writing. Write down whatever comes into your head about the event you are remembering.

8. Keep practising! Writing is just like learning to play a musical instrument. You need to keep practising.

Glossary

adjective describing word that tells you about a noun or naming word

appointment time and date of something that you need to do on a particular day

blog type of diary that you write online on the internet

chronological the order in which things happened

first person you are writing in the first person if you are using 'I' or 'we'

formal language that is correct and follows the rules

informal language that is more friendly and breaks some of the rules

introduction opening few lines of a piece of writing

non-fiction writing that is about real people or things

online connected to the internet

paragraph more than one sentence, grouped together

past tense form of a verb that describes something that happened in the past

pronoun word that stands for a noun or naming word

recount writing that describes events in the past

sentence group of words that makes sense on its own

time connective joining word or words that shows when things happen or happened

timeline way of setting out events in the order in which they happened

verb doing or action word

Find out more

Books

Getting to Grips with Grammar series, Anita Ganeri (Raintree Publishing, 2012)

Rip the Page! Adventures in Creative Writing, Karen Benke (Trumpeter Books, 2010)

Websites

www.bbc.co.uk/schools/ks1bitesize/literacy

www.bbc.co.uk/schools/ks2bitesize/english/writing

Index